Dustin Grinnell

The Velvet Ghetto

Dustin
Grinnell
The
Velvet
Ghetto

Blue Cubicle Press, LLC
Plano, Texas

The Velvet Ghetto

Copyright © 2023 by Dustin Grinnell

Published by
Blue Cubicle Press, LLC
Post Office Box 250382
Plano, Texas 75025-0382

ISBN 978-1-938583-56-8
Library of Congress Control Number 2023941392

Printed in the United States of America.

Front Cover by Nora Kelly

Dedicated to all those who say aloud
what everyone is thinking.

Contents

Introduction

Maybe it's my New Hampshire origins—my strong identification with the state's motto, "Live free or die"—or my somewhat troubled relationship with authority, but I often bristle at being told what to do and exactly how to do it, especially in the workplace. I grow frustrated when candor among colleagues is frowned upon and I must self-edit for sensitivity beyond the typical needs of diplomacy and tact.

So, when a marketing department for which I worked as a writer brought in authoritarian, deceptive, hypocritical leaders who sought to promote conformity and stamp out individuality, I wasn't happy. I might've been earning a respectable income at a supposedly prestigious organization, but there was a palatable erosion of self over time, and I began to feel like a corporate drone living in a velvet ghetto.

A collection of twenty-five poems, *The Velvet Ghetto* explores the complex emotions I felt while working in that toxic environment. Knowing others around me felt as I did but were too afraid to speak out for fear of retribution, these poems use first-person plural pronouns. This book is our hate letter to Corporate America.

When I finally left that job, I wrote a scathing resignation letter and emailed it to the whole department, burning bridges with everyone, including some coworkers with whom I'd become friends. I stole the email's subject line from the movie *Jerry Maguire*: "The things we think and do not say." This collection attempts to put into words the things we think while working for corporations but find difficult to say.

This experience wasn't my first run-in with the ills of Corporate America. In the decade I've worked for American corporations, I've witnessed mindless bureaucracy, rampant conformity and groupthink, brutal office politics, sickening hypocrisy, and illiberalism, all symptoms of totalitarian systems that deprive people of their dignity, integrity, and humanity. It's disturbing to see the rise in corporate power in the United States. Broadly speaking, corporations essentially enslave their laborers within hierarchical systems that, in many environments, demand blind obedience.

Yet this is the devastating reality of capitalism, according to the linguist, writer, and philosopher Noam Chomsky. "It's ridiculous to talk about freedom in a society dominated by huge corporations. What kind of freedom is there inside a corporation? They're totalitarian institutions—you take orders from above and maybe give them to people below you. There's about as much freedom as under Stalinism."

To be fair, the indignities many suffer in American corporations typically result not from overt malice but from uncritical bureaucrats following orders—"good soldiers," like the content manager mentioned in this book. Even if their conduct violates their conscience, they can justify it through rationalization: "I'm just doing my job."

This attitude speaks to the phenomenon Hannah Arendt refers to as the "banality of evil"—the terrifying apathy rational individuals can exhibit when involved in or witnessing something unjust. Indeed, "when you think of the long and gloomy history of man," wrote scientist and novelist C. P. Snow, "you will find more hideous crimes have been committed in the name of obedience than have ever been committed in the name of rebellion."

Working in that toxic department and experiencing hypocrisy, deception, and authoritarianism, I felt like a young

Che Guevara, as portrayed in the movie *The Motorcycle Diaries*. After witnessing inequality and human suffering during a year of travel across South America, Guevara refuses to return to his normal life, instead taking his first steps toward the revolutionary he would later become. At the end of the movie, Guevara tells his friend, "So much injustice."

These words resonate with me. This book resulted from a need to put words to the injustices people working in Corporate America could inflict on each other. While Guevara would eventually choose bullets as his weapons, I choose words. I hope these words shed light on toxic corporate behavior, shame those who treat others badly, and inspire us all to avoid such behavior in the future.

It is no measure of health to be well adjusted to

a profoundly sick society.

—Jiddu Krishnamurti

They call it "9 to 5." It's never 9 to 5 . . . . And what hurts is
the steadily diminishing humanity of those fighting to hold jobs
they don't want but fear the alternative worse. People simply
empty out. They are bodies with fearful and obedient minds. The
color leaves the eye. The voice becomes ugly. And the body. The
hair. The fingernails. The shoes. Everything does.

—Charles Bukowski

I would rather be a devil in alliance with truth, than an angel
in alliance with falsehood.

—Ludwig Feuerbach

The Velvet Ghetto

The Propagandists

We are the organizational storytellers:

The communication experts controlling the narratives.

We waste our best years elevating brands,

Trading our talents for money,

Instead of investing them in novels or poems.

Skilled in the dark arts of dressing up corpses,

Of putting lipstick on pigs,

We spin the negatives and play up the positives.

We promote the services, spotlight the initiatives, and sell the products.

We are our companies' spin doctors:

The propagandists.

Cubicle

We promised we'd never inhabit a cubicle:

A small, windowless box with no natural light,

Where we'd stare at unnaturally glowing displays

For eight hours a day, five days a week.

Yet with a promotion,

The promise is broken.

As our leader guides us from cubicle to cubicle,

Past the offices of those higher up on the chain,

We are offered any cubicle we desire,

As if such a choice was an honor.

It looks like a prison,

Which we say aloud.

When we receive a puzzled look in return,

We realize we mustn't talk so darkly

While we're among the institutionalized.

Every day, we rearrange symbols in software,

Sitting in the same chair,

Tapping on our keyboards.

From the third-floor office's only window,

We gaze out onto a busy square.

Our eyes flit over the pedestrians we find there,

Like hummingbirds around a feeder.

Yet more like songbirds,

We are caged.

Over time, we become restless and disillusioned.

We visit the gym to decompress after work.

In spin class, we bounce up and down for sixty minutes.

After, we sprawl on the couch for hours on end.

Can we really complain?

When money is secure?

We should be grateful for the security of salary and insurance,

For a stimulating job in a stimulating city at a stimulating
workplace.

But we are overstimulated, and our bodies are just along for the
ride.

Through it all, we only live from the neck up.

If we don't make a change,

Our bodies might rebel.

Life Sentence

We finish our work by two or three,

But we cannot leave until five,

So we surf the web

Or chat with coworkers,

And by the end of the workday, we're exhausted.

We are miserable.

Our skills don't match our responsibilities,

Or our abilities exceed our jobs.

Many are burned out.

Others are "bored out."

Alienated from our work and selves,

We are melancholy.

Maybe we have side hustles that offer the promise

Of better, more authentic lives.

We make beer or cookies

Or candles and sell them

And dream of turning them into businesses.

But we don't follow through.

Sometimes we think about changing careers,

But we'd have to go back to school.

That would take time.

That would take money.

Neither survives loans, children, and work.

What went wrong?

We did what we were supposed to:

College, good career, climb the ladder.

But it feels like a hoax.

It feels like a trap.

We threw everything in, and now we can't get out.

It's a life sentence.

The Velvet Ghetto

Prestigious institutions offer us respectable incomes,

But what do they demand in return?

Obedience,

Conformity,

Individuality stamped out.

We're white-collar slaves to bureaucratic leaders.

What can we do but what we are told?

Otherwise they'll show us the door.

Show them obedience,

Artificial identities,

Insincerity as civility.

We're corporate drones living in a velvet ghetto.

Retirement

Friends and family fan the flames of our angst:

They could never live like us!

Living in the same city,

Reporting to the same building,

Taking orders from some boss,

Day in and day out.

How can we stand it?

We say we will do what we want in retirement,

But to them, such waiting is repugnant.

Saving things for our sixties

Is mortgaging our future.

It's postponement.

It's procrastination.

It's death—an early death.

Chain of Command

Every week during staff meetings, our leader presents

Our growing department's organizational chart.

It's a game of "fill the open positions."

The large screen displays the evolving chain of command,

A top-down hierarchy of roles and responsibilities.

Our leader is at the top.

We are near the bottom.

The "org chart" shows who still needs to be hired,

But the regular display to the anxious group reinforces

An inflexible, hierarchical culture

Of uneven power distribution.

The Hotshots

During the restructuring, our leader poaches

A seasoned executive from a similar organization.

With her, she brings her top two lieutenants,

A trio of hotshots, assembly-line efficient.

Together, they build a small army around them

Of similarly minded workers—a tight-knit bunch.

They create their own subculture within our department,

with team-building meetings and their own Christmas parties.

They leave people cold with ambiguous rhetoric

Littered and laced with corporate jargon.

Skilled as they are in bureaucratic jujitsu,

They never break rank and always cover their asses.

It doesn't take long for us to realize

The authoritarian tendencies in their everyday actions.

Obedience without question is what they demand,

Even when time frames might make tasks impossible.

They adjust their own deadlines with flexible ease,

Yet they extend such grace to no one else.

They champion their own ideas, while others' are suspicious,

And truth and reality are regularly distorted.

If a project goes amiss, they scapegoat the vulnerable,

Operating with impunity whenever problems arise.

When not occupied with tasks, they busy themselves

Talking about barbecues, babies, and ball games.

Those who think freely or prefer to be honest

Are thorns in their sides, pains in their necks.

Their orders and deadlines aren't realistic, we say,

And we suggest new approaches to assignments.

But even minor departures from their original visions

Are insubordination by their interpretation.

They're not impressed with our avant-garde creativity,

And they shun our desire for innovation in work.

They can't fathom our refusal to uncritically submit

To the reign of the hotshots over our department.

Better Opportunities

Restructuring invited in authoritarian leaders,

Who built an oppressive environment,

A culture of fearful obedience.

Employees begin resigning for "better opportunities,"

Neglecting to tell anyone the truth,

Assuming the knowledge would do no good.

The issues are so pervasive, the department can't be reformed,

Only abandoned in favor of "greener pastures."

In their wake, the authoritarians act with impunity,

Against which we lack the courage to speak,

So we stay and suffer in silence.

Paranoia

Our leader implements quarterly meetings

With every employee in the department.

These allow employees to talk about themselves

And express any concerns they might have.

We use these meetings to provide useful feedback

And attempt to diagnose cultural problems,

But we sense others use them to inform on each other

And undermine those with whom they clash.

Our leader asks about our positions,

Our career goals, and personal lives,

She rummages, too, for interpersonal conflicts,

Small problems that threaten to grow big.

Her intentions seem true and based in concern,

Yet her questions only sow paranoia.

Woke, Inc.

The hotshots send out an email of "importance,"

A new policy to adopt in the workplace:

Latinx for Latin American people,

Despite the offense that it causes Hispanics.

We've always been quick to support and fight for

Equality, freedom, diversity causes,

Yet we struggle to keep up with the new program,

Our company's DEI manifesto.

We've got questions, concerns, doubts to contend with.

We want the perspective of those represented.

But company culture won't let us speak freely,

Inquisitiveness has been banned and restricted.

We don't know exactly the reasons for this

But we censor ourselves and just say what we need to.

In groupthink we fall as we try to keep up with

The ways that the business philosophy changes.

We fear if we don't, if we aren't "woke" enough,

We'll find ourselves objects of loathing.

Hypocrisy reigns where the most "woke" among us

Are commonly privileged white folks.

This ideological capture is happening everywhere

In media, government, healthcare.

Employees who strongly connect with agendas

View those who do not "walk the walk" with suspicion.

Their righteous approaches are almost religious.

Their fervor concerns us, alarms us, scares us even.

Such zealots can often be hostile and threatening

To people considered to be nonbelievers.

Corporate Values

Our leaders have called for new company values:

Display "passion and curiosity" in our work.

Yet how can these values become our reality

When curiosity and passion have always been shunned?

Our leaders just want all the projects done quickly

And in accordance with their demands.

We've gotten in trouble when displaying these traits,

Yet now we must adopt them for the sake of the company.

Innovators

They say they want innovators, pioneers, and explorers.

It sounds good in theory, but innovators are pains in the ass.

We question what everyone has come to rely on,

And view the status quo as a thing of the past.

We seek to reform what we see as outdated,

Compulsively trying what others have not.

The changes we seek, it turns out, are unwanted.

For months, we try making a place for ourselves here,

But soon we consider seeking a new home somewhere else.

We do not find comfort in the culture they have here,

And they're only comfortable without us around.

Troublemakers

Our leaders say they want creative employees,

With imagination, tech savvy, and high emotional intelligence.

The left side of the brain is as important as the right,

And empathy for others is all the rage in corporations.

Yet a factor that our leaders do not realize or accept

Is that the ideas that such employees typically put forth

Can be path-breaking, irreverent, downright impractical.

They hire us because we have the qualities they "want,"

Passionate and curious, never thinking within the box.

But soon we're idealistic, cavalier, and way too honest,

Impulsive and romantic, impolitic and even crass.

Our leaders didn't realize that the source of good ideas

Can also question their authority and, more, the status quo,

Or those strong imaginations might begin to want reform,

undermining existing values or the standards they uphold.

Our leaders start to wonder if they've hired troublemakers.

If we continue to rock the boat, they might throw us overboard.

The Bureaucrat

The new content manager seems to play well with others,

Yet we find her unpleasant when no one's around.

She equates the results of our "thinking different"

With acts of disrespect and insubordination.

We quickly resent her aversion to risk

And tactless, insensitive critiques of our work.

She's quick to dismiss the ideas we suggest

Yet seldom has original ones of her own.

The indifference she shows is invalidating,

More upsetting to us than outright rejection.

In meetings, she's vulnerable to groupthink,

Agreeing with the majority for political expedience.

She blindly submits to our leaders, who love her,

And conforms to their every whim.

For us, though, there's more to managing projects

Than controlling their flow, which is her primary role.

We want to contribute in meaningful ways,

But how, when each project makes us feel less appreciated?

Her style is soulless, her managing punitive.

In emails, she indicates we've ignored her instructions.

She provides us with feedback in punishing terms

and constantly searches for examples of misconduct.

She makes it her mission to correct our behavior,

To prevent aberrant activities from becoming "a pattern."

She demonstrates the danger a bureaucrat can present

When they question nothing in following orders.

Shame

A heavy atmosphere fills the halls of Corporate America.

What is this thick feeling in the air?

It's shame.

Shame for how the conditions have made us behave.

Shame for participating in mindless bureaucracy.

Shame for acting passive-aggressively.

Shame for gossiping and wounding reputations.

Shame for bullying the least powerful among us.

Shame for conforming and not thinking for ourselves.

Shame for agreeing with others because it's expedient and safe.

Shame for being who we've been.

Shame for occupying our place in the world.

Antihero

We used to be well-liked by most colleagues,

Team players who pitched in to help.

We'd often go above and beyond,

Maintaining a positive attitude.

But authoritarians flooded our workplace,

With administrators and ideologues too.

The heroes within us began to shrivel,

Leaving critics with bad attitudes.

This turned us into rebels who called people out

On bullshit they weaved day to day.

We became antiheroes.

Problems With Authority

The bureaucrats brand us: authority problems.

We are dysfunctions, outside of their order.

They focus on making us play by their standards.

They marginalize us when we don't obey them,

Or ridicule us or imply termination.

They label us narcissists, sociopathic.

Such retaliation keeps us from speaking out.

The threats keep us fearful, submissive, and hiding.

Yet faced with such hypocritical nonsense,

We constantly waver from option to option:

To keep our mouths shut and forfeit our integrity,

Or speak up and suffer the consequent backlash.

Illegitimate Authorities

Can it be said that we have problems with authority

When we've never had such problems before?

We have had bosses in the past who were smart, capable, sincere,

Whose spaces were egalitarian in atmosphere.

Together, we'd discuss strategies and who to hire.

They gave respect and we returned it.

Their orders we obeyed.

Our problems come with illegitimate authorities:

Those who are incompetent, oppressive, untrustworthy,

Who exist only to preserve existing power structures.

If they were legitimate, we'd have no issues.

They brand themselves as democratic and of open minds,

Yet they aren't interested in collaboration.

In dealings day to day, it's servitude they expect.

With every project, they demand that things be done their way.

And yet none of them ever do any of the work.

They administrate and manage us with just their words.

Radicalized

Worse injustices exist than corporate oppression.

We know this.

But hypocrisy, oppression, and deception changed us,

Radicalized us.

We must fight for those who have suffered indignities,

Do something.

Activists and dissidents and revolutionaries,

We read them.

We learn that mindful change doesn't come from those in power,

But from below.

We must find the courage to speak up if something's wrong.

Can we?

Speaking Up

We write a memo about how unsafe we feel psychologically.

We find the courage to say we work in a toxic culture.

We inform our leader and send it to her.

She assures us our job is secure,

But from what we've seen of this authoritarian culture,

We're certain our words will get us fired.

Disgruntled employees have complained before

And were let go without explanation.

Yet to our surprise, conditions get better,

Our memo has made a change.

The bureaucrat's deadlines become manageable,

Her feedback less critical.

The feeling of oppression we've sensed for so long

Has lifted and eased in its wake.

These positive developments came from us speaking up,

A watershed moment for us.

We weren't marginalized or punished or terminated

When confronting authoritarian leaders.

We spoke our minds to those above,

And we found that things improved.

It bolstered our sense of self-worth and integrity.

Perhaps we found an identity.

The Beautiful Mess

As our leaders suggest, we meet with a career coach,

Who creates a space to talk and reflect.

It becomes fertile ground for self-discovery,

Insights for meaningful ways to perceive ourselves.

This leads us to a more positive self-understanding.

We make lists of our values and who we admire.

We consider how we can best use

Our idealism and creativity in corporate culture,

We perform introspective practices that

Get us in touch with the emotions we're feeling.

We discuss the ones we experience most often

In Corporate America, like anger.

Anger, we learn, has many underlying sources,

Being ignored, disempowered, humiliated.

Perhaps our personality and temperament

Aren't suited for bureaucratic hierarchy.

Perhaps it'd be better to work for an organization

With a less hierarchical structure.

Maybe we should work in a creative department

That welcomes new ideas, not looks at them with suspicion.

And yet we feel drawn to, paradoxically so,

The absurdities in the bureaucratic system.

We're shaking things up here in the big, beautiful mess,

Challenging systems and fixing what's broken.

Invalidation

The longer we work with our content manager,

The more flummoxed we become.

Our ability to communicate with her

Seems hindered at every turn.

If we say the scope of a project is

Too large for the time proposed,

She'll imply we don't work fast enough

Or don't support the team

When we have too many assignments

And not enough time to finish them,

We're dramatic and unprofessional.

Such matters, she says, are her domain,

Not open for discussion.

She refuses to tolerate

Our questioning of the rules she lays down.

The reactions she has to our requests

Invalidate our positions,

As though we're acting out in anger

Instead of being reasonable.

Under control of tyrannical leaders

And inflexible managers,

What does invalidation like this

Do to rational people?

It drives us to rebel.

We know we must leave.

Resignation Letter

On our last day, we'd like to share our views

To a department of toxicity and silence.

This has become an authoritarian system

That favors blind submission to those in power.

It discourages free-thinking individuals,

Demanding and rewarding obedience instead.

Innovative thinking is considered

Insubordinate and disrespectful.

Bureaucrats and project managers are praised for their work,

While creatives and idealists are marginalized.

Our leaders created a totalitarian system

That exploits workers within its strict tiers.

The main source of oppression are the hotshot employees

and teammates who do their bidding, unthinkingly:

Lack of imagination, nonsensical bureaucracy,

Oppressive directives and lifeless efficiency,

Bourgeois values, moral cowardice,

And ass-kissing, conformist culture.

Our leaders brand themselves as open-minded and democratic,

But day to day, they exercise dominance over employees.

They justify their behavior as "just doing their jobs,"

But that is a mindless excuse for bad behavior.

Dominating employees through bureaucratic channels

Causes more injustices than overt criminal behavior.

We find it absurd that we're urged to talk

About inequality and fairness in general.

How can we discuss national or global injustices

When we can't even admit to anyone else

The indignities we suffer every day at the hands

Of an invalidating, soulless work environment?

Democratic, we became a problem for our leaders,

Authoritarians who expect uncritical obedience.

They crush dissent through disciplinary actions

And swift and unexplained terminations.

Do such tyrants not understand that the "problems"

We create for them are deliberate?

They are acts of resistance to maximize free speech

And minimize oppression for those at the bottom.

How long can a department last when it's built on

Exploitation of labor fueled by fearful compliance?

How long will people work under the conditions,

Where projects are all "my way or the highway"?

Like capitalistic systems that regularly boom or bust,

Our department's oppressive culture created an unstable system.

We considered trying to reconcile through frank conversations,

But we're not allowed to "get real" in our department.

It's impossible to relay our side of the story

Or discuss matters in context, with nuance.

Instead, conversations must stay unnaturally "professional,"

No addressing genuine conflicts or meaningful changes.

Others, we know, suffer in silence,

Unwilling to stand up when they'll only be knocked down.

We sense the anguish they feel when they start their workdays,

The spiritual pain of producing in fearful submission.

We feel empty when we dump propaganda on the internet

Because we produce it without a sense of purpose.

Our culture has no mission, no identifiable soul.

It alienates us from our work and from ourselves.

We urge those who stay to

Talk with one another—from the heart.

Talk about the oppression and unburden yourselves.

Change won't come from leadership, not from above.

It must come from you, from within and below.

Recovery

We commit to our health, almost radically so,

In sleep schedule, water, and food.

We meditate daily and do yoga often,

And cease working on weekends to rest, instead.

Open weekends encourage our minds to play more,

Which sets the stage for creative spurts.

The influx of ideas we record on our phones,

Raw material for creative projects.

To deal with emotions, we begin a routine

Of walking out our frustrations.

When emotions well up that are strong, intense,

We stay with them as we work through them.

Resolution or not, we've acknowledged our feelings,

A walking therapy session.

Loving Our Fate

Our escape from Corporate America was not complete,

But our new job's culture is open-minded, democratic, flexible.

The organization was founded on creativity, innovation, and bold action.

We work well with our new teams and begin to thrive.

We embrace the work as a solid foundation,

A day job to support our more fulfilling creative work.

Its ready-made purpose keeps our feet on the ground

As we navigate uncertainty in our creative life.

It provides security from money worries,

And feeling secure fuels creative projects.

Meanwhile, we search for a metaphor

That can help us navigate our lives.

We once imagined ourselves as Sisyphus,

Endlessly, pointlessly, rolling a boulder uphill.

Yet such a metaphor no longer fits

How we feel about our lives.

Instead, the metaphor we choose for now

Is Nietzsche's notion of "loving one's fate."

Everything that's happened has contributed

To who we are now and what we're doing.

We're both limited by our circumstances

And free to pursue what we find meaningful.

We're restricted by our places in life

And free to transcend them.

This is the compromise of living a human life.

Though we aim for fulfillment and more than we have,

We accept where we are and who we are right now.

This is our life,

So let us love it.

Dustin Grinnell is the author of *The Genius Dilemma*, *The Empathy Academy*, and *The Healing Book*. He holds an MFA in fiction from the Solstice MFA Program at Lasell University, an MS in physiology from Penn State, and a BA in psychobiology from Wheaton College (Massachusetts). He grew up in the White Mountains of New Hampshire and lives in Winthrop, Massachusetts. Learn more at dustingrinnell.com.